AF731721

DIARY OF A MINECRAFT ZOMBIE

BOOK 21

CARNIVAL CHAOS

Copyright © 2022 Zack Zombie Publishing

All rights reserved. No part of this publication may be reproduced, distributed, or transmitted in any form or by any means, electronic or mechanical, including photocopying, recording, scanning, or by any information storage or retrieval system, without the prior written permission of the publisher, except in the case of brief quotations embodied in critical reviews and certain other non-commercial uses permitted by copyright law.

This unofficial novel is an original work of fan fiction which is not sanctioned nor approved by the makers of Minecraft. Minecraft is a registered trademark of, and owned by, Mojang Synergies AB, and its respective owners, which do not sponsor, authorize, or endorse this book. All characters, names, places, and other aspects of the game described herein are trademarked and owned by their respective owners. Minecraft ®/TM & © 2009-2022 Mojang.

ISBN 978-93-5471-839-7

This reprint edition April 2026

Printed In India at Shivam Offset Press, New Delhi

DIARY OF A MINECRAFT ZOMBIE

BOOK 21

CARNIVAL CHAOS

BY

Zack Zombie

TUESDAY

'EXTRA, EXTRA! READ ALL ABOUT IT! CIRCUS COMING TO TOWN AND THERE'S NO DOUBT ABOUT IT!'

'Since when have we had newspapers in the Overworld?' I asked Creepy as we headed down the street towards school.

'Dunno, but did you hear that?! A circus!' Creepy flipped the newspaper mob a Coin and grabbed one off him.

'Look! "Boogeyman's Big Top is coming to town. This circus has received RAVE REVIEWS and is sure to be a hit!"'

Creepy read aloud. 'Man, I love the circus.'

'I didn't know you'd been to a circus before,' I said.

'I haven't. I just love the idea of a circus. I'd love to be in one someday.'

I leaned over his shoulder to look at the newspaper. 'I think you can.' I pointed at the second paragraph of the story.

Boogeyman's Big Top is doing something unique. They will be holding **AUDITIONS** *next Monday for locals to take part in the circus' final show. Contestants must come prepared with all their own equipment, and the three best performances will be* selected to take part in the greatest circus of all time—Boogeyman's Big Top!

'Whoa,' Creepy and I said at the same time.

'What would you do?' I asked Creepy, already running through possible acts in my head.

'I dunno. Maybe I'll **JUGGLE...**'

I paused. 'Creepy, you don't have arms. How will you juggle?'

'HSSS. You'd be surprised how good I am with my feet!'

'I'M HOOOOOOOME!' I yelled as I slammed the front door shut and dumped my backpack at the foot of the stairs.

Wesley's babysitter popped out of the living room. 'Oh good, you're home. I'm off then.' And she dashed past me out the door.

Weird. Why was the sitter here when Mom was off work? I shrugged. It had been a long, hard day at school and my **PEA-SIZED** brain was tired. It needed a snack.

I headed towards the kitchen. 'Mooooooooooom! Is there cake?'

No reply.

'MUUUUUUUM!!'

Still nothing.

Then I heard a soft moan.

I followed the noise to Wesley's bedroom and saw an **ENTIRE WATERMELON** on the floor.

Well, what was left of an entire watermelon.

Wesley was lying on the bed, his belly bulging.

'Hey, buddy, you okay?' I asked.

Wesley let out the helpless groan of someone too **FULL** to talk. He tried to roll onto his stomach, but gave up halfway. He grunted again.

'Alright then.' I shrugged and left his room, closing the door behind me.

'MUUUUM!' I called again.

Still no reply.

Well, if mom wasn't home it meant I could eat whatever I wanted, right?

I went downstairs and found an **ENTIRE CAKE** in the fridge.

YEEEESSSSS!

Half an hour later I was lying on the couch, groaning from being too full. It occurred to me that maybe Wesley had had the same thought I did.

Later I heard the front door open and close, followed by a *thunk!*, as someone dropped a bag near the foot of the stairs.

'MILDRED?!'

My dad's thumping footsteps echoed down the hall as he followed Wesley's **MOANS.** Pretty soon after that I heard him come back down the stairs.

I groaned too, so he would come into the living room without me having to get up.

'Zombie?' My dad found me on the couch, unmoving.

I grunted in reply.

'Well,' I heard him say to himself. 'If Mildred isn't home, I can eat whatever I want, right?'

Oh no.

Half an hour later, my dad was sprawled on the floor next to me, the last crumbs of an **ENTIRE PUMPKIN PIE** scattered around him. He tried to roll onto his side, but struggled and finally gave up.

I wondered if I should remove my stomach so it didn't hurt me anymore.

Too. Much. Food.

'It's okay, Zombie,' my dad puffed. 'Your mother will be home soon and she'll **FIX US UP.**'

I nodded slowly and looked at the clock. It was pretty late though.

Where was Mom?

WEDNESDAY

I woke up, still on the couch.

Dad was still on the floor, but Wesley was tottering around the living room.

'**BREAKFAST?**' he asked.

'Sure,' I said, as I pushed myself upright. 'Mom will make us some.'

I looked around. The place was still a mess from last night.

'MUUUUUM!' I yelled.

Nothing.

I leaned over and shook my dad awake. 'Dad. DAD! Mom still isn't here.'

Dad sat up with a **GRUMBLE** and looked around groggily.

'Huh?'

'Mom isn't back and Wesley and I want breakfast,' I repeated.

'Sure, sure. I can make breakfast. How hard can it be?'

Dad stood up and stumbled to the kitchen, yawning and stretching. Wesley waddled after him and I lay back down on the couch. Just five more minutes...

CRASH!!

CLANG!

BOOOOM!!

I jumped up and ran into the kitchen. It was a disaster zone—stuff was everywhere, and not in a good Zombie house kind of way.

'Uhhh,' Dad said slowly.

'Uhhh,' I agreed. I didn't know what else to say.

'**PIZZA?**' Wesley suggested.

'Great idea—pizza!' Dad went to the freezer and rummaged around to find one. 'Ah-ha!' he said proudly, handing a couple of frozen slices to me and Wesley.

Frozen? I shrugged and started eating.

When we were done eating, I asked, 'What about lunch for school?'

Dad glanced around the kitchen and his eyes landed on the rest of the pizza. 'Here you go, son. **LEFTOVERS!**'

I looked blankly at the leftover pizza and then back at my dad. 'When's Mom coming back?'

Dad looked nervously around the kitchen. 'I dunno, son... Hang on, aren't you guys late for school?!'

'Guys?' I asked. Then I understood. 'Dad, you know Wesley doesn't go to school, right? He's not old enough yet.'

Dad's **EYE HOLES** widened. If he could have, I think he would have started sweating. 'Right. I knew that. Adventure time for me and Wesley, huh, buddy?'

Wesley didn't look impressed.

'Are you having cold pizza for lunch?' Skelee asked. 'That's so cool! I wish my mom would let me have pizza for lunch. I've got beetroot again.' Skelee sighed.

We had a party at my house a while back and Skelee got obsessed with a beetroot. His mom figured that if she made him eat beetroot for every meal he would get over it. It must be working.

'Trust me, you don't,' I grumbled. It was very soggy now.

'Guys, I have a plan for the circus audition,' Creepy announced.

'Whatcha gonna do?' Slimey asked through a mouthful of peanut butter sandwich.

I eyed his sandwich and **DROOLED** a little.

'I am going to...' Creepy paused for dramatic effect, **'SING!'**

Our lunch table was silent.

'Sing?' I asked eventually. 'I didn't know you could sing. I've never heard you sing in my life.'

'Life?' Skelee asked.

'Death? Deathtime?' I suggested. 'Whatever.'

'HSSS. I've been having singing lessons ever since I was shorter. I've definitely mentioned this,' Creepy hissed.

'Sing us a song then!' Skelee said.

Creepy smiled. Phew!

He stood up, cleared his throat and started to **YELL.**

I immediately clapped my hands over my earholes. Skelee's bones began to shake. Slimey seemed to shrink.

Look... let's just say it **WASN'T GREAT.** We definitely need to break the news to him before he tries to audition.

THURSDAY

When I came down for breakfast there was still no Mom. But there was Dad with a **FRILLY APRON** and frying pan.

'BREAKFAST, SON!' he yelled at me.

'Ow, why are you yelling?'

'WHAT?'

'WHY ARE YOU YELLING?!' I shouted back at him.

'OH, SORRY. THE SMOKE ALARM WENT OFF SO MANY TIMES IT MAY HAVE DAMAGED MY HEARING

A BIT. NO WORRIES, EAT UP!' Dad dropped a plate of **BURNT** pancakes in front of me.

'Umm...' I started.

'OH, OF COURSE, YOU WANT SYRUP!' He rummaged around in the cupboard. 'HMM, THIS LOOKS LIKE SYRUP.'

Before I could say anything, Dad tipped a thick black goo all over my pancakes.

Weird. It didn't look like syrup at all. I shrugged and shoved a massive piece of syrupy pancake into my mouth. Dad would know, right?

WRONG.

I spat it back onto my plate. 'WHAT IS THAT?'

I grabbed the jar and read the label: BLACKSTRAP MOLASSES. What even is that?!

BLEUGH!

'Dad, that is disgusting!'

'WHAT?' He squinted at me and then at the plate of pancakes.

'Oh, never mind.' I picked up my backpack and headed for the door. Just as I was leaving I heard Dad coughing and spluttering.

He must have tried the

BLACKSTRAP MOLASSES.

'Where's Mom?' I asked when I got home from school.

'Uh, not here. Want pizza?' Dad opened a box of steaming fresh pizza.

'Alright.' I scooped up a piece and started munching. Mmmm, **HOT PIZZA** at last.

'I have a surprise for you kids,' Dad said excitedly.

'Is it Mom?' Wesley asked.

'Uh, no.'

'Is Mom coming back soon?' I asked.

'Uh, no.' Dad looked stressed again. 'But I've got us **TICKETS** to see the circus!' He waved three big, colorful tickets in front of us.

'Ooh, yeah! That sounds fun!' I said, and Wesley clapped his hands excitedly.

'Great! It's starting soon, so gobble up that pizza and we'll go.'

It was bright and colorful and there were mobs everywhere. Dad made us hold onto each other so we didn't get lost as we pushed our way to the entrance.

They scanned Dad's tickets and we filed into the massive **BIG TOP** tent and found our seats.

'Now, kids, be prepared. The circus may have some wacky stuff,' Dad whispered to us.

Suddenly the lights went out and a hush fell over the mob crowd.

Then a **SPOTLIGHT** flashed on and a Skeleton with a cape, top hat and cane walked into the light. He spoke in a booming voice:

'WELCOME ONE, WELCOME ALL TO BOOGEYMAN'S BIG TOP! THE BIGGEST, MOST EXCITING, MOST RIVETING, MOST ENTERTAINING, MOST EXQUISITE, MOST...'

I looked at my watch.

Five minutes later, he was still going. '... MOST TANTALISING, MOST ENTRANCING, MOST RIVETING—'

'YOU ALREADY SAID THAT!' a mob from the crowd shouted.

'UHH...' The ringmaster looked thrown off. 'MOST... TALENTED! YES, **TALENTED** CIRCUS YOU WILL EVER SEE! WE HAVE DEATH-DEFYING TRAPEZE ARTISTS, LOOSE-LIMBED CONTORTIONISTS, TREACHEROUS

FOOT JUGGLERS, CREEPY CLOWNS, OCELOT TAMERS, AND OTHER ACTS YOU'VE NEVER SEEN THE LIKE OF!'

'Ooh.' Wesley leaned forward in anticipation.

'SO WITHOUT FURTHER ADO...'

'**FINALLY**,' my dad sighed.

'PLEASE WELCOME THE HUUUUUUULA HOOPING SLIIIIIIIIMES!'

The Skeleton bounded out of the ring and three Slimes appeared with a hula hoop around each of them.

'Is this a real circus trick?' I asked my dad. 'We hula hoop in P.E.'

'I'm sure it's different. It must be a higher degree of difficulty,' Dad said confidently.

It wasn't.

For seven minutes we watched in silence as three Slimes tried to hula hoop. I **CRINGED** the whole time.

The ringmaster came out again. 'WASN'T THAT INCREDIBLE?!'

No one clapped.

'NEXT UP IS THE DEATH-DEFYING TRAPEZE ARTISTS! PUT YOUR HANDS TOGETHER FOR OUR BIGGEST STARS!'

Suddenly two mobs swung into the middle of the Big Top from nowhere!

One was a Zombie and the other was an Enderman.

They flew through the air, swinging and flipping, catching and throwing each other. They were **AMAZING!**

Everyone was on their feet, cheering and whooping as each leap got harder and harder.

At the end, they both landed on their tiny platforms near the top of the Big Top circus tent.

And for a second, the Zombie artist looked like...

No. It couldn't be.

I almost thought for a second...

For a second, she looked like **MOM.**

THURSDAY, LATER

I thought that trapeze artist was Mom, but I must have been wrong. Dad was clapping really hard, but that was just because they were so good, and Wesley didn't notice anything.

The rest of the circus was pretty good. I was **STOKED** to try out for a part with them.

After we got home, Dad patted us both on the head and said, 'Alright, off to bed!'

'But I've got **HOMEWORK,**' I moaned.

'Oh.' He looked at the time and then at me. 'It's a bit late. Why didn't you do it earlier?'

'Uh... cause as soon as I got home you told us we had to leave for the circus,' I said.

'Ah. Alright, go do your homework now then.'

'But Dad... it's Math. Mom usually helps me with Math.'

'Oh... does she?' Dad looked nervous. 'Well, I guess I can help you out...'

We sat at the dinner table and I pulled open my textbook with a *THUMP!*

'Wow. It's a **CHUNKY** one, huh?' Dad said as he tried to pull the heavy textbook towards him.

I nodded and got out a pencil and worksheet. Then I looked at Dad.

He stared back at me.

'This is the part where you help me,' I explained.

'Oh, right! Well, what's the problem, son?' Dad asked. 'Seven plus three? Seven minus three? Seven *times* three? Those multiplications always get me.'

'Um, we're doing **FRACTIONS**.' I pointed at the heading in the textbook.

'Fractions?'

I tried to explain. 'Yeah, you know... one number on top of another number, with a line in the middle...'

Dad stared at me blankly, then at the page I had open.

'You know what, son? How would you like to **GET OUT** of homework? I'm sure you're tired and want to go straight to bed. You're no use at school with no sleep! I'll write a note for your teacher.' Dad patted my head. 'Now off you go. And don't forget to dirty your teeth before bed!'

Alright! No homework! This is the best!

FRIDAY

'I swear, my dad said he would write me a note—he must have forgotten. But he told me I could skip homework! Otherwise I would be too tired for school.'

I could hear the snorts and laughs from the other mob kids as I tried to defend myself to Ms. Bones.

'Yes, and I saw an **ENDER DRAGON** on my way to work this morning.' I think Ms. Bones would have rolled her eyes if she had any. '**DETENTION.**'

'Ughh!' I walked back to my desk next to Creepy.

When I sat down, I realized he was humming to himself.

Loudly.

Oh man, this was gonna be a long class.

I made it through all my classes with Creepy humming to himself without stuffing a sock in his mouth. When he joined me and the guys for lunch, he had just come in from singing to a tree in the playground 'for practice'. He was still **HUMMING.** Maybe I should use that sock...

'If Creepy is doing it, I want to sign up for the circus too!' Slimey said.

'Me too!' Skelee chimed in.

'Hey, do you want to do something together?' Slimey asked.

'That's a great idea!' Skelee nodded happily. 'What should we do? I was thinking a balancing act. I have a great center of gravity.'

'I don't know what that is, but I like the idea of a balancing act... OH! Why don't you ride a **UNICYCLE** while I balance on your head?!'

'What are you gonna do?' Creepy asked me in a pause before he started humming the chorus.

I shrugged. 'I dunno. I saw the circus though. My dad took me and Wesley after school.'

'Really?!' Creepy finally stopped humming to himself. 'What was it like? Was it magical?'

'Um... not the word I'd use. The mobs on the trapeze were pretty amazing though. But if they start to show the hula hooping Slimes—run.'

'Hey!' Slimey said defensively.

'Dude, trust me. You don't want to put yourself through that.'

'Annnnyway,' Creepy said, 'we're all auditioning so you gotta do *something* for the circus!'

'Hmm, maybe I'll do

ACROBATICS?'

'Can you do a handstand?' Skelee asked.

'Oh man, I'm a **PRO.'** I jumped off the bench, then knelt down, put my hands on the ground and kicked my legs up into a perfect handstand.

Or at least that's what I thought I did.

The guys thought I barely hopped off my feet for a second and said my legs definitely didn't go up over my head.

'Hmmph,' I grunted. 'Fine. I'll just have to think of something else!'

The bell rang.

Great, a whole lot more humming to get through and after that— detention. **SIGH.**

There was an unexpected surprise waiting for me in detention.

When I walked into the sad, dingy classroom, there was one other student there.

ENDARIA!

Endaria's mom and my mom were friends from way back. They stayed with us for a while after the Aliens destroyed their hometown, and liked it so much they decided to stay for good.

'Hey! What are you doing here?'

Endaria shrugged. 'Turns out the new principal doesn't like it when you borrow her **PIG** and ride it around the playground.'

'DUDE!' I said in awe. 'That is awesome.'

'What can I say? It's hard to turn down a **DARE.**'

At that moment, Mr. Blaze, the history teacher, floated in and sat down at the desk at the front of the classroom. I cringed, waiting for him to start yelling—he is always getting angry, Mr. Blaze.

'Okay, you two mobs. This is detention for me just as much as it is for you. So sit there quietly and do your homework, and we all get to go home at the end of the hour.' Then Mr. Blaze leaned back in his chair and shut his eyes.

Huh. Endaria and I looked at each other, then back at Mr. Blaze.

He **SNORED.**

'So, how have things been for you? Has your mom forgiven you for trashing the house yet?' Endaria chuckled.

While Endaria and her mom were staying with us, I had thrown a massive party to try and impress her, but the mob kids trashed the inside of the house and some Pillagers trashed the outside so Mom had wanted to boot me into another Biome. I hadn't seen Endaria since then, cause Mom had grounded me for a month.

I swooned a bit—her laugh still made me want to **THROW UP,** in a good way.

'Zombie?' Endaria asked.

Oh right, focus. 'Yeah, she is past it... I think. Well, I dunno to be honest.'

Endaria looked confused. 'What do you mean?'

'I think my mom's gone missing. I haven't seen her since breakfast on Tuesday. But it's strange cause Dad doesn't seem too fussed.' I paused before deciding to just say it. 'I went to the circus with Dad and Wesley, and, I know it's weird, but I think I saw my mom there.'

'What? Like, watching the circus?'

'No,' I shook my head. 'On the trapeze. It looked so much like her! But I must be **WRONG**, cause Mom doesn't know how to do trapeze and Dad totally didn't recognize her. I'm probably just imagining things.'

Endaria looked very creeped out.

'No. Way.' Endaria said loudly. 'ME TOO!'

Then she remembered Mr. Blaze was sleeping, and darted a quick look at him. He was still snoring.

Now it was my turn. **'WHAT?'**

'I haven't seen my mom since breakfast Tuesday either. Heather Huskly's mom picked me up Tuesday after school and said I'd be staying with them for a while. Then I went to the circus and I think I saw my mom too,' she whispered.

'Where?' If I had a heart, it might have been pounding really fast at that point.

'On the **TRAPEZE!'** Endaria hissed. 'With your mom!'

SATURDAY

'Steve!'

THUMP!

'STEVE!'

THUMP!

'STEEEEEEEEEEEEEEEEEEEVE!!' I yelled as I ran into the clearing where Steve was punching trees.

'**WASSUP,** dude? How's it hanging?' Steve threw another punch at the tree.

'Fine, but also very *not* fine,' I panted. 'I need your help, this is **URGENT.**'

'Is this about your audition for the circus? Creepy told me about it. Also, why is Creepy singing? Someone needs to tell him he sounds like a Pig when a mob pulls its tail.'

'True, but it's not about that!' I grabbed Steve by the arm, then looked around to make sure no one was nearby to overhear. 'My mom went missing and I've just worked it out—she's been kidnapped. BY THE CIRCUS!'

'What?!' Steve couldn't believe it.

'Yeah! I went to see the circus and I'm **ALMOST SURE** I saw her there. And Endaria's mom is also gone and she thinks she saw *her* at the circus too! They must have been kidnapped by the circus and now they're being forced to perform as trapeze artists! It's the only thing that makes sense! Steve...' I took a breath. 'I need you to help me get her back.'

'You're almost sure?' Steve asked.

'Almost positive!' I confirmed.

'Well in that case, yeah sure... but how?'

'I have a plan. We're going to **INFILTRATE** the circus.'

'Infiltrate?' Steve asked.

'Yup! We're gonna sneak in and liberate her.'

'Liberate?'

'Yes, free her. Keep up, Steve!'

'I know what those words mean, Zombie, I just didn't think you did. You know, with your pea-sized brain and all.' Steve gestured at my forehead.

'I didn't pay any attention at school Friday, so I've got all my **MENTAL FOCUS** stored up. We're gonna sneak into the circus and free my mom!'

'Okay... do you have any idea *how* we're gonna sneak into the circus?'

I grinned at Steve and pulled a long coiled whip from my backpack.

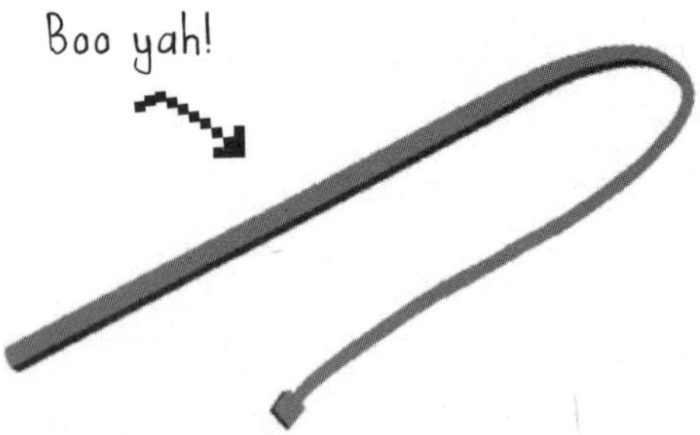

'Uhhh... what is that?' Steve asked nervously.

'It's part of my plan!' I said proudly.

'You need a **WHIP** to sneak into the circus?'

'Yup! Because to sneak into the circus, we're gonna audition with the best circus act *of all time!*'

I paused for dramatic effect.

Steve squinted, so I think the pause was working.

'**HUMAN TAMING!**'

'Human taming?' Steve raised an eyebrow. 'That doesn't seem right.'

'Not real Humans, silly. *You* are the Human! And *I'll* be the heroic Human Tamer!'

Steve didn't look impressed.

'Don't worry, I'm just gonna *pretend* to tame you!' I said quickly. 'And you'll be totally safe amongst all those mobs cause they'll be coming to watch a circus! It's the perfect plan, really. No fear!'

'Pfft, I eat **DANGER** for breakfast!' Steve said, puffing out his square chest. 'Alright, let's do this! You think this will get us into the circus long enough to find and free your mom though?'

'Definitely.' I gave him a thumbs up.

'I'm hoooome!,' I yelled.

'Hi, son!' Dad called back.

I followed his voice into the kitchen to find him unpacking grocery bags.

'Look!' he said proudly, gesturing at all the food he'd bought. 'Now you can have a *real* lunch for school again! And dinner too!'

'Cool,' I said as I started to rummage through the bags looking for snacks. I found a box of **COOKIES**, tore it open and dug in. 'Cookie?' I offered Dad the box.

'No, thanks.'

I quickly scanned the kitchen and living room. 'Is Wesley in his room? I'll give him a cookie too.'

'Wesley...?' Dad paused.

'Yeah,' I said slowly. **'WESLEY.'**

'Wesley,' Dad repeated.

'Wesley.' I nodded.

'GET IN THE CAR, NOW!' Dad bolted from the kitchen and grabbed his car keys.

'Dad?!' I asked, following him.

'DAD!'

Dad flew into the driver's seat and I jumped into the passenger seat, buckling my seatbelt.

'Dad, what's going on?!'

Dad sped out of the driveway and down the street towards the grocery store.

'Oh man, oh man! Your mom is gonna **CLEAN** me!' Dad was mumbling to himself.

'What's going on?'

'I forgot Wesley. I think I left him at the grocery store.'

Oh boy. Even I know that's not good. On a scale of *good parent* to *room for improvement*, forgetting your mob kid at the grocery store is definitely on the '**IMPROVEMENT**' end of the scale.

When we finally got to the grocery store, we started searching through the aisles, but the shop was too big. We had to find the store manager and ask for help.

The manager was a Creeper with a tag pinned to his vest that read, 'Chris'.

'Hi, how can I help you?'

'Uhh, I think I lost my kid here,' Dad said. 'His name is Wesley. He's a Zombie, about yay high.' Dad held his hand against his leg to show how small Wesley was.

'Oh. Yes. I know *exactly* who you're talking about. HSSS.' Chris's face shifted from polite smile to annoyed frown. 'Please follow me.'

Chris led me and Dad through a 'STAFF ONLY' door and into an endless **MAZE** of back corridors. Finally he showed us into an unmarked room. And there was Wesley.

'Wesley!' Dad picked him up and hugged him close. 'Sorry I lost ya, kiddo!'

'Ahem,' Chris cleared his throat. 'In the time you left the young Zombie here unsupervised, he caused a bit of **DAMAGE** to the store. HSSS.'

'Oh...?' Dad said slowly.

'Please take a seat.' Chris gestured at some chairs in front of a screen.

Dad and I sat down, and Chris pointed a remote. The screen came to life and, clear as day, we could see Wesley...

Ripping open boxes of cookies, knocking over a tall stack of apples, pocketing marshmallows, rotten candy and dried booger flakes, stuffing himself on whole watermelons. He looked like an Ocelot gone **WILD.**

He had gotten through at least three quarters of the watermelon before a security guard found him. And when the guard reached down to pick him up, he wiggled, slipped out of his grasp and scuttled away. Chris hissed behind us.

The video cut to a camera that pointed at the deli, where a whole bunch of roast chickens were on display. Wesley jumped onto the counter, grabbed a roast chicken and started to **RIDE IT** around the store.

Well, 'ride it' is a stretch. Wesley straddled the roast chicken, and dragged it around. I guess he couldn't understand why it didn't run like his Chicken at home did. You can't blame a Chicken Jockey, really.

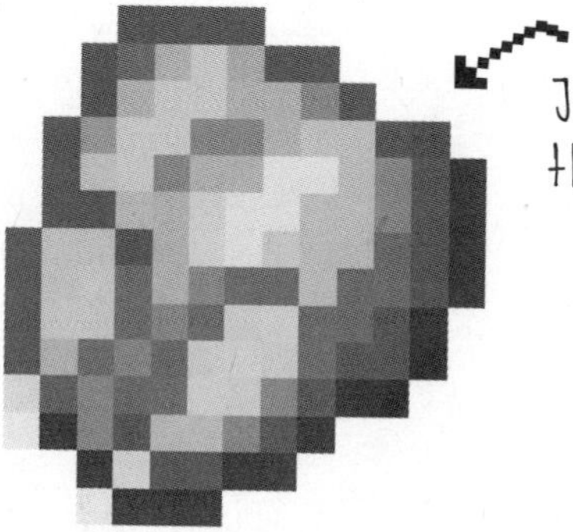

Just not the same

I looked at Wesley, happily munching on **MARSHMALLOWS** he was pulling from his pocket.

'Haha, wow.' Dad nodded sheepishly. 'The kid sure got up to a lot!'

'Yes. Yes, he did,' hissed Chris.

'I'm sorry for the damage. I'll cover the costs.' Dad sighed and pulled out his Coins.

SUNDAY

Steve pointed at me. 'Okay, here's the plan. We practice our routine, get it **PERFECT**, and then at the audition tomorrow we absolutely smash it.'

'YEAH, SMASH IT!' I cheered.

'Then we can save your mom.'

'WOO!' I gave Steve a high five. 'Dude, we really need my mom back. Dad is just not coping. He left Wesley at the grocery store on Saturday.'

'Oh man. Was Wesley okay?'

'Yeah, he had a great time riding the **ROAST CHICKENS** around. The shop mobs weren't too happy though. Dad had to buy them all. We're gonna be eating roast chicken for weeks.'

'Sometimes I'm glad I don't have parents. I mean, sure, sometimes they sound great, but sometimes they sound like too much work,' Steve said.

'I used to think it would be fun to have no mom. No rules, no chores, eat whatever I wanted. But turns out everything really falls apart without her.'

'Wow, that's **DEEP.** Maybe you should thank her when we rescue her from the circus,' Steve suggested.

'Yeah,' I said. 'That's a good idea. "Hi, Mom. Me and Steve saved you, you're welcome! Also, thanks for being my mom." Pretty good, hey?'

'Suuurre,' Steve replied. 'Okay, let's practice our Human Tamer act. First, put that whip away. I have a better idea.' Steve pulled out a stick from behind his back.

'A stick?'

'No, a **STAFF!**'

'What's a Staff gonna do?'

'Dude, the Staff is gonna make it look like you're making me do things. You know, like a **MAGIC MOD.** Trust me, it'll be great,' Steve said excitedly.

'Alright, alright.' I grabbed the Staff off Steve and started to wave it around.

Huh, this is pretty fun. Steve might be on to something here.

MONDAY

'COME ONE, COME ALL, TO THE AMAZING, ASTONISHING, ASTOUNDING BOOGEYMAN'S BIG TOP! AUDITIONS THIS WAY!'

I nervously walked through the crowd, pushing Steve in a Minecart.

He had practiced his best **BLANK** stare yesterday, and it looked great. Real Zombie-ish actually.

There was a huge **CROWD** in front of the Big Top. Every mob and their Zombie Horse was there.

'What in tarnation?! Is that you, Zombie?' Old Man Jenkins marched over leading his Zombie Horse, Dumpling.

'Hi, Mr. Jenkins,' I said. 'You and Dumpling are auditioning?'

'Why, I thought we oughta. It seems like the best place to show off dear ol' Dumpling's tricks.' He leaned close and whispered, 'Just between you and me, she's a pretty talented ol' gal!'

Then Old Man Jenkins noticed Steve. 'What on the Overworld?! Is that a *Human?!*'

'Shhh! Keep it quiet, Mr. Jenkins. I don't want anyone to **PANIC.** But trust me, he's totally safe. Look!' I poked Steve in the face.

Steve didn't move.

Old Man Jenkins totally fell for it. 'Well, lookee here. A **TAME HUMAN.** Who woulda thought!

You've done a pretty crazy thing there, young fella.'

'Yeah, thanks Mr. Jenkins,' I said as I started to push Steve and his Minecart away.

Once we were far enough from Old Man Jenkins and everyone else, Steve swung around. 'DUDE!' he shout-whispered. 'What did you poke me in the face for?!'

'I had to. To prove you were totally **SAFE** and under my control!'

'Yeah, well, it wasn't fun on my end! Maybe just poke me in the arm or something next time.'

'Won't that make your arm fall off?'

Steve just gave me a look.

'Oh right, Human. Sorry, my bad.'

Suddenly a bell rang. The Skeleton ringmaster strode out. 'HELLO EVERYONE! WELCOME TO BOOGEYMAN'S BIG TOP! PLEASE TAKE A NUMBER AND WE WILL CALL EACH OF YOU! ONE! BY! ONE!'

I pushed Steve's Minecart up against the side of the Big Top and told him to stay.

Steve looked like he wanted to throw me into water and watch me grow real skin. Eugh, **ITCHY.**

I shrugged. Oh well.

I went to the counter and collected a ticket.

127.

Oh man, 127 already? It's gonna be a long day...

'125! NUMBER 125!' the Skeleton ringmaster called.

'Almost us, Steve!' I said, trying to keep **MORALE** up.

He just grunted from his seat in the Minecart. His legs were hanging over the side.

'Dude, what is going on?!'

I looked up and saw Creepy, Slimey and Skelee walking towards me and Steve. 'Hey, guys! You all set for the auditions? What numbers did you get?'

'Never mind that. What is Steve doing here?!' Slimey asked, while Creepy hissed loudly.

'Shhhh!!' I hushed them quickly. 'No one can know that Steve and me are friends. He's part of my act!'

'YOUR ACT? You're auditioning with him? What can a Human do?' Skelee asked.

'Hey!' Steve said.

'Sorry, but you know what I mean. Everyone can punch a tree.'

'Not everyone,' Slimey said sadly. Creepy nodded.

'Whatever, you know what I mean,' Skelee said, rolling his **EYE-SOCKETS.**

'126! NUMBER 126!' the ringmaster hollered.

'We're next!!' I nudged Steve. Then I turned back to the guys. 'Guys, you can't say anything to anyone here. Everyone has to think I have tamed Steve and put him completely under my spell.'

'Okay, sure.' Creepy shrugged.

Steve pulled his feet back into the Minecart and sat up straight, assuming his blank stare again.

'Ready.'

'Okay.' I opened my backpack and pulled out a **TOP HAT** I had found in the back of Dad's cupboard, as well as the whip.

Steve looked at me. 'I thought we agreed no whip?'

I nodded sheepishly. 'It's just for show. You know, to set the mood.'

Steve raised his eyebrow at me.

'I promise! I'll put it down as soon as you are revealed, and use the Staff, like we practiced.'

Then I pulled a big black sheet out of my backpack and threw it over Steve.

Now it just looked like a covered stack of **BLOCKS** in a Minecart.

'127! NUMBER 127!' the ringmaster called.

'Okay, remember Steve, still as blocks,' I whispered.

'Good luck!' the guys called after us.

I pushed Steve through the massive tent flaps and into the Big Top.

It was **PITCH BLACK,** but a spotlight beamed down on a microphone in the middle of the circus ring.

I wheeled Steve to the edge of the spotlight, but left the black sheet over him. Then I walked up to the microphone. 'Hi, my name is Zombie.'

SILENCE.

I didn't know who I was speaking to. The spotlight was shining so brightly it blinded me, making the audience completely invisible. I swallowed.

'Uhh, this act will be... uh... unlike anything you've ever seen before.' I paused again, but there was no response. I shut my eyes and tried to convince myself this was no different to our rehearsals.

I grabbed the microphone off the stand and walked back to Steve, still covered with the sheet. 'This act is the show of a real **HERO!** Watch me as I put my life... uh, I mean death, on the line, to tame the most dangerous, the most threatening, the most hostile mob in the Overworld!'

I yanked the sheet off and Steve sprang out of the Minecart, roaring.

I heard gasps from the edge of the circus ring. 'A HUMAN!'

So someone was there! And my 'Steve reveal' impressed them! I dropped the whip, quickly pulled my Staff out of the Minecart and waved it in Steve's direction, shouting '**ABRACAZABRA!**'

Steve went still.

With a few waves of my Staff and some fake magic words, Steve performed trick after trick, just like we had practiced. Some were basic tricks, like pretending to be some other mobs, and others were really tricky, like jumping through a **BURNING HOOP.** We figured only a really tamed Human would do that!

At the end of the performance I took a bow, and then waved my Staff and commanded Steve to take a bow as well.

When we straightened up again, a single mob was clapping. It echoed in the empty Big Top.

The spotlight dimmed and the rest of the Big Top lights came on.

The mob clapping was standing near the edge of the ring. There were three other mobs sitting in the first row with clipboards, taking notes.

'I like this act. Put them on the list,' the clapping mob announced. Then he swept away, exiting through a door I hadn't noticed before.

'Sure thing, **MR BOOGEY,** sir,' called one of the mobs with the clipboards. But he was already gone.

It was only when we were outside the Big Top, and Steve had given me a high five before heading off for home, that I realized what that clapping mob was.

I thought they were only in fairy-tales, but clearly not.

Mr. Boogey? That mob was obviously **THE BOOGEYMAN!**

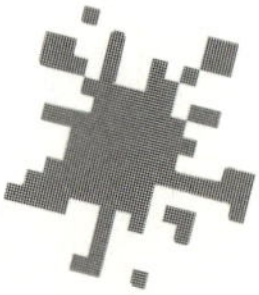

TUESDAY

'Hey Dad, can I **SKIP SCHOOL** to go to the circus to rehearse my performance? Okay, cool, thanks!' Before Dad could reply, I grabbed my backpack and bolted out of the house.

'Circus?' I heard him say to himself as I shut the front door behind me.

I was a couple blocks away when I found Steve hiding in a bush, next to a Minecart.

'Dude, what are you doing?' I asked.

'I don't have a costume! I need to be **INCOGNITO.**'

'What's cognito?'

'No, *incognito*. It means you blend in. Like a spy!' Steve explained. 'I need you to push the Minecart again so mobs don't try to... you know.' Steve mimed shooting an Arrow, then crossed his eyes and flopped to the ground.

'Yeah, yeah, okay I get it.' I walked around to the Minecart and Steve climbed in. He put on his blank stare and lolled his head to the side. I started pushing him along the street.

'Okay, so the plan for today is recon,' I muttered under my breath to Steve. 'We're gonna scope the place out, avoid the Boogeyman—'

'Wait, what? The Boogeyman?' Steve laughed. 'That's not real, it's a **FAIRY-TALE** to scare the kids. You gotta stop watching so much TV.'

I glared at Steve. 'While you were busy pretending to be a tame Human, I was keeping my eyes open for clues. The mob that clapped us at the audition, that signed us up? He was the **REAL LIVE** Boogeyman!'

Steve looked at me doubtfully.

'Anyway, as I was saying, we scope the place out, see what's going on and find a way to sneak my mom out.'

'What about Endaria's mom?'

'Yeah, her too. Anyway, the final show is tomorrow, so we gotta be sure and we gotta be quick. If we don't free the moms by tomorrow, they'll be packed up with the rest of the circus, the Boogeyman will take them away and we'll never see them again!'

'Don't worry, Zombie.' Steve turned around and gave me a thumbs up. 'We'll find the moms.'

'WELCOME! YOU MUST BE ZOMBIE, **THE HEROIC HUMAN TAMER,'** the ringmaster shouted at me.

'Yeah,' I said, rubbing where my ears should be. 'Where should I go?'

'JUST WAIT BACKSTAGE UNTIL YOUR ACT IS CALLED,' he replied.

I pushed Steve **BACKSTAGE...** into a crowd of other performers. Most were the regular circus mobs, but some were locals who had auditioned like Steve and me.

'Dude, this is perfect. Let's have a look around,' I whispered to Steve.

Steve slowly got up and we quickly blended right into the crowd. We snuck around the back and found a hallway that led to the dressing rooms.

'This way!' I pulled Steve into a dressing room, grabbed some **GREEN MAKE-UP** and smeared it all over Steve's face.

'Hey! I'm not a dancing clown, you know,' Steve hissed at me.

'Well, you said you wanted to be incognito!' I hissed back.

'Dude, look!' Steve grabbed me by the shirt and pulled me behind the dressing room door. We hid as two creepy looking clowns walked down the hallway, talking.

'And then Larry got out of the car, and then Pete got out of the car, and then Carl got out of the car,' one clown sighed. 'It's fine to cram us all in there, but I wish they'd tell the new mobs to stop **FARTING** in the car.'

'I know, right? It's only polite!' The other clown nodded. 'So many clowns, so many farts.'

'How good are those trapeze artists, huh? I can't believe ol' Boogey found them so last minute.'

'He's talking about my mom!' I whispered to Steve. 'I was right, the Boogeyman does have her!'

Steve nodded and hushed me.

'Yeah! Those mobs are pretty impressive. I wonder if they'll be staying on **FOREVER...**'

Forever?

What?!

No way! We absolutely need to **RESCUE** my mom!

We couldn't hear the rest of the conversation cause the two clowns were now walking away from us. Steve and I eased out of hiding. He wiped the green off his face and then noticed the panicked look on my face.

'Don't worry, Zombie! We'll get your mom back!' Steve patted me on the shoulder, nearly making my arm fall off.

Just then, Old Man Jenkins and Dumpling came around the corner. 'Zombie! Zombie's Human! What are you two fellas doing back here?'

'Nothing!' I said quickly. 'Just practicing.'

'Alrighty then. Me and ol' Dumpling here are just taking a walk to stretch our legs. Lot of **WAITING AROUND,** bein' in a circus. I think you're up soon for rehearsal though!'

'Oh, thanks Mr. Jenkins!' I said. 'We should get out there to make sure we don't miss it. Come on!' I prodded Steve, who had dropped his head down like a **PUPPET** without strings when Old Man Jenkins showed up.

Steve and I headed back to the main backstage area to wait to be called.

'Dude, we gotta figure out a way to rescue my mom before the circus packs up and takes her with them forever!' I said to Steve.

'Zombie, I think I've got an idea,' Steve said slowly. 'But... you're gonna have to trust me on this. It's gonna be **BIG.**'

WEDNESDAY

I stepped out on stage, with Steve still in the shadows. Suddenly everyone in the crowd started **LAUGHING.** Their laughs got louder and louder until they filled the big auditorium.

No, not an auditorium; the Big Top. The curved, tented ceiling rose high above me as the sound of cackling laughter filled it.

Why was everyone laughing?

I turned back to look at Steve and he was laughing, too. He wasn't pretending to be a tame Human anymore. In fact, Steve was laughing so hard that he fell to his knees and clutched his stomach. Then he **POINTED** at me.

Who, me?

Why?

I looked down and realized... I wasn't wearing any clothes! In front of everyone!

Awwww, man!
Not naked!

I looked around in a **PANIC.** I could see everyone I knew in the crowd laughing at me: Dad, Wesley, Skelee, Creepy, Slimey, Endaria, Mom, Old Man Jenkins—

Wait, Mom? Mom was here? And she was safe! Out of the evil clutches of the Boogeyman! I was so happy to see her I forgot where I was for a minute.

Then I tuned the laughter back in and remembered I was still on stage, **NAKED.** I turned to run backstage, but then I realised there was no backstage! I was on a high, round platform where everyone in the crowd could see me.

I was panicking now. I started to run in circles. How do I get off the stage? How do I get off the stage?

'AAAAGHHHHH!'

I woke with a jolt from the worst daymare ever.

Today was the big performance and I was super nervous. I don't even know how I was nervous—it's not like I have any **NERVES.**

Just don't think about it, I told myself.

I got myself ready on auto-pilot, and met Steve by the bush so I could push him to the circus in the Minecart.

'Dude? Dude!' Steve tried to get my attention by clicking his fingers in front of my face. I looked at him numbly. 'Snap out of it! You gotta focus. The plan is **FOOL-PROOF**; everything will be fine.' I immediately felt better. Steve was right. We got this! No way the Boogeyman is gonna win.

We got to the circus and stood backstage with everyone else. That's when I saw Creepy, Skelee and Slimey and guiltily waved at them. I had been so busy worrying about my mom that I hadn't even checked to see how their auditions went.

'Hey, guys! I'm sorry, I didn't even ask you about your auditions. But you got through! That's great!' I said. Then a thought hit me. 'Hang on, how come I didn't see you at rehearsal yesterday?'

'Oh, we didn't get through,' Creepy explained. 'We just snuck backstage to see you and Steve before your big performance! Good luck, guys, you're gonna **SMASH** it out there!'

'Ha,' I laughed nervously. 'If you only knew.'

I checked the listing of who was going on in what order, and saw Steve and I were performing last. We were the **BIG FINALE.**

'Wow,' I muttered to Steve. 'The Boogeyman must have been really impressed!'

Steve didn't answer. He was sitting in the Minecart next to me, in full tame Human mode.

I'd been on the lookout for the Boogeyman, but I hadn't seen him since my audition. Which I guessed was kinda the point—you don't see him until he's *got* you. My mom wouldn't have stood a chance.

I suddenly felt nervous again. *We got this*, I reminded myself.

I snuck a peak from behind the backstage curtain. The Big Top was filled to the brim with mobs who had come to see the infamous Boogeyman's Big Top. It was **SHOWTIME.**

The ringmaster started shouting an insanely long opening speech, rambling on and on and on, just like when Dad brought us to watch the show.

Finally the first performance of the night was up. It was the **LOOSE-LIMBED CONTORTIONISTS.** I watched from the sidelines as a group of Zombies filed out into the circus ring in an orderly manner and began performing. One bent over backwards and popped her arms out of their sockets so her head touched the floor. Another popped his head off so a third could balance on his shoulders.

I swallowed nervously and began pacing back and forth.

'What on the Overworld is going on? You look like a Sheep that swallowed a Cactus!'

I turned to see Old Man Jenkins and Dumpling standing behind me. Dumpling had been brushed so much she shone.

'I'm just nervous,' I said. 'I'm sure I'll get over it... or else I'll **CONK OUT** and Steve will get all my drops. Could go either way really.'

'Who's Steve?' Old Man Jenkins asked.

'Uh, I mean, my tame Human,' I stammered, patting Steve on the head. Oops!

'Aww shucks, young man. It can't be that bad. Lookee here, you were good enough to get through the audition, so you must have a **STELLAR** performance.'

Dumpling neighed in agreement.

'Maybe,' I nodded doubtfully.

'Just remember, this is all a bit of fun. People come here for fun and they come to see fun. No one is taking anything super-duper serious. Me and Dumpling are just here for a wacky ol' time!' Old Man Jenkins gave Dumpling an encouraging whack on her hindquarters and Dumpling neighed in surprise.

'AND NEXT UP,' the ringmaster shouted, 'IS MR JENKINS AND HIS ZOMBIE HORSE, DUMPLING!'

'Alrighty, **BREAK A LEG,** young fella.' Old Man Jenkins patted me on the head, then led Dumpling out into the circus ring.

I watched as Dumpling ran in circles. Then Old Man Jenkins started throwing steamed dumplings at her while she ran and Dumpling leapt in the air and caught each one in her mouth. Then Old Man Jenkins climbed onto her back and, as she rode in circles, slowly, bit by bit, he stood up on Dumpling's back. Then she started **GALLOPING** at full speed.

I didn't even know she could run that fast.

Eventually Old Man Jenkins finished his routine and I cheered loudly from backstage while he bowed to the clapping crowd. Old Man Jenkins walked out of the ring, and everyone congratulated him on his performance.

There was so much **FUSS** that I almost didn't hear the ringmaster announce the next performance.

'AND NOW WE HAVE THE MOST MAGNIFICENT, AWE-INSPIRING, DEATH-DEFYING TRAPEZE ARTISTS YOU HAVE EVER SEEN!'

That was my mom!

STILL WEDNESDAY, TWO MINUTES LATER

The trapeze artists performed the same routine I had seen when I came with Dad and Wesley. It was just as great as last time and the rest of the audience loved it as much as I had. After they ended with a **MASSIVE FLIP,** the audience stood and cheered loudly.

I got ready to grab her as she exited. I had to tell her not to worry, that Steve and me had a plan. But Mom exited the ring on the opposite side to me. Oh no, I was going to lose her!

I tried to push my way to the other side of the ring backstage but kept running into mobs. It was so crowded and everyone was in costumes.

Suddenly I heard, 'AND NOW FOR THE TREACHEROUS FOOT JUGGLERS!'

A herd of Creepers **RUSHED** past me, flexing their feet and carrying balls in their mouths.

I got swept up with them, but at the last moment an Enderman **STAGEHAND** grabbed me, saying 'Get back here! You're not a Creeper!' He pulled me backstage again, and shook his arm at me angrily.

By then Mom was gone.

I trudged sadly back to my side of the ring backstage and found Steve.

'Dude, don't leave me again. I got some really weird looks when you left me alone,' Steve whispered to me. 'One of those Creepers started glowing when he saw me!'

'Sorry, man,' I muttered. 'I thought I saw my mom. We're gonna have to rescue her really soon.'

'Don't worry. There's no way the plan will fail.'

After a few more performances, it was almost our turn.

'Are you **NERVOUS?**' I asked Steve.

'Nah,' he said confidently. 'I've been preparing for this my whole life. You?'

'Pretty nervous. If I was a Creeper, you'd have a heck of a lot of gunpowder right now!'

'PUT YOUR HANDS TOGETHER FOR THE CLOWNS AND THEIR CAR! NOW, FOR THE FINAL PERFORMANCE, WE HAVE... DRUMROLL PLEASE... THE HEROIC HUMAN TAMER!'

A **GASP** went through the crowd.

I froze. Suddenly, some stagehands were pushing me and Steve out into the ring. At the last second, a microphone was thrust into my hand and that was it.

I was out in the ring alone.

Just like my **DAYMARE.**

I turned back to see Steve hidden in the shadows, the big black sheet draped over him. I looked at the microphone and cleared my throat. Feedback squealed through the Big Top and I could make out the mobs in the audience wincing.

Oh boy, this was already ten times worse than auditions. And about on level with my daymare.

'Hello,' I said awkwardly into the mic. 'Humans are the **WORST** mob in the Overworld. Would everyone agree?'

A half-hearted cheer came from the audience.

'They build, and they destroy and they just generally annoy! They are the most dangerous, most mysterious mob ever known. And right here, right now, I have one completely under my control.'

Another gasp went through the crowd and I could hear them shifting nervously.

I walked back to where Steve was hiding, just outside the spotlight, and gently pushed the Minecart into the light.

'**BEHOLD!**' I whipped the sheet off with a flourish and Steve jumped out, roaring at the crowd!

Some mob screamed in fright, and a murmur rippled through the crowd.

I cracked my whip once, just for show. Then I dropped it and grabbed my Staff.

'Abracazabra!' I shouted. Steve went still.

'This Human is completely under my control!' I turned to Steve, held up a hoop and waved my Staff again. 'I **COMMAND** you! Jump through the hoop!'

Just as we rehearsed, Steve looked around slowly, just enough to make the audience more nervous, but then he obeyed and jumped through the hoop.

I gave another few basic commands and Staff waves and Steve paused and then followed through on each one.

Then I looked at Steve and I gave him a wink—**THE SIGNAL.**

'Human! Get down on the floor and lay on your back for a belly rub.'

Steve paused, looked left and then looked right. He slowly began to lower himself onto one knee.

Then he stopped. And slowly stood again.

'No,' Steve said.

'What? Human, I command you! Abracazabra! GET DOWN!' I waved my Staff at Steve frantically.

Steve **CACKLED** and then ran at me.

I dropped the Staff, turned and started to run in the opposite direction, with Steve giving chase.

When I was near the edge of the ring, I turned and dodged back around Steve. He **ROARED** again and ran past me towards the crowd.

Mobs in the crowd shrieked and with thundering feet they started evacuating the Big Top while Steve ran around lunging at them. The panic swelled and grew and suddenly the exits were overflowing as mobs tried to push their way out.

I slipped backstage where it was absolute **CHAOS.** Everyone there also wanted to escape the crazy Human.

CRACK!!!

I stopped and peeked back out into the main ring again and saw one of the poles holding up the Big Top tent had a massive crack. The crowd were stampeding around it, trying to get out.

Suddenly, a hand grabbed my arm. I jumped, then breathed a sigh of relief when I saw it was only Old Man Jenkins and Dumpling. I'd thought for a second the Boogeyman had got me!

'What in tarnation are you doin' standin' around?! We gotta get outta here!' Old Man Jenkins shouted, and rushed away, leading Dumpling by her reins.

Just then, I saw what I was looking for. Two trapeze artists in amongst the backstage crowd.

'MOM!'

STILL WEDNESDAY, FIVE SECONDS LATER

'Zombie?' Mom turned at the sound of my voice and ran back towards me. 'Zombie, what are you doing here?!' She grabbed me in a big hug. 'It's not safe! There's a Human on the loose!'

'Don't worry, it's only Steve. We're here to RESCUE you! Come on!' I grabbed her by the hand and started to pull.

'Steve?' Mom shook her head, confused, but she didn't budge. 'Sounds like you have some explaining to do, young Zombie!'

'Mom, we gotta go while the Boogeyman is distracted!' I shouted and pulled her harder.

'WAIT!' she said, holding fast and not moving.

'What?!' Then I understood and smacked my forehead with my palm. 'You're right! Endaria's mom! We need to rescue her, too. Quick, grab her and then we can go!'

'Rescue?'

Suddenly a loud siren blasted through the Big Top. I covered my earholes and looked up at the speakers. That's when

I noticed the very high ceiling suddenly didn't seem all that **HIGH** anymore.

'THE BIG TOP IS COMING DOWN!' a Skeleton screamed as she ran past us. The crowd surging towards the backstage exit became a lot more frantic.

'We gotta go! Endaria's mom is probably already out!' I grabbed Mom's hand and pulled again.

Just then, Steve popped up at my side. 'Hi, Mrs. Zombie! Time to go!'

Steve pulled a small tub of green paint out of his pocket and started to smear it on his face and arms. He had already changed into a turquoise shirt and purple pants. Full Zombie **DISGUISE!**

Then Endaria's mom appeared. 'Mildred, what's happening? We need to evacuate now.'

'Yes, we do!' I said. 'Keep your heads low so no one notices you in the crowd.'

Mom looked like she wanted to argue with me, but didn't have the chance cause we got swept up in the rush out the exit.

By the time we got outside, the Big Top was **DEFLATING** like a jumping castle at the end of a birthday party.

Steve and I had stayed together, but it took us a minute to find the moms again. Once we did, Steve patted me on the back and said to my mom, 'It was lovely seeing you again, Mrs. Zombie! Congratulations on being freed. Sorry I can't stay to celebrate—gotta go before anyone spots me!' Then Steve **SLUNK OFF** into the bushes and out of sight.

'ZOMBIE!' I heard a bellow and turned to see Dad running towards us, carrying Wesley.

'Dad! Look! I rescued Mom from the Boogeyman!' I pointed at Mom.

'Rescued Mom from the Boogeyman? What are you talking about?' Dad asked.

I stared at him. 'Didn't you notice that Mom went missing? I did some investigating and found out that the

Boogeyman from Boogeyman's Big Top circus had **KIDNAPPED** her and Endaria's mom and was making them perform on the trapeze. So Steve and me hatched a plan to rescue them. But we gotta go now before the Boogeyman realizes we snuck them out in all the chaos!'

Dad looked very sheepish. 'Oh no. Did I forget to tell you? Oh boy.'

'Francis!' Mom said angrily. 'Zombie, honey, I didn't need saving. I was with the circus because I wanted to be!' She glared at Dad. 'Your dad just forgot to tell you, I think.'

'But Dad didn't know where you were either,' I said, confused.

Dad looked even more guilty. 'Well, I knew she was with the **CIRCUS,** I just didn't know where the rehearsals were being held. Sorry, I obviously wasn't very clear.'

'But, why were you with the circus if you weren't kidnapped?' I asked Mom.

'Well, Eloise and I used to do the trapeze together when we were in school.' Mom gestured at Endaria's mom. 'We were catching up for a coffee when Mr. Boogey, who is a **ZOMBIE** just like us, overheard us talking about it. His trapeze artists ran away from the circus just before the show was due to open here, so he was in a bit of a bind. He asked us to perform and we agreed. It was something I wanted to do for myself.'

'Oh... so the Boogeyman didn't kidnap you? You were never in any danger?' I felt kinda **STUPID.**

'No, but I can understand why you thought so. Thanks for coming to save me.' Mom smiled and gave me another big hug.

I turned back to the massive, deflated Big Top.

'So I did that for **NOTHING?'**

'Umm...' Mom paused. 'Yes.'

'We should leave,' Dad said with a lowered voice. 'Before anyone works out it was us.'

THURSDAY

I found Endaria at school and told her all about the Big Top performance and how our moms weren't really kidnapped. She didn't seem **SURPRISED.**

'Yeah, I know,' Endaria said. 'My mom came to get me from Heather's after the show last Friday. She told me all about it.'

'What?! Why didn't you tell me?!' I slapped my palm on my forehead.

Endaria looked confused. 'I thought you would just ask your dad about it. I never realized you would think she had been kidnapped and forced to perform at the circus.'

I blushed. When she said it like that, it did sound a bit **OVER THE TOP.**

'Oh well,' I said. 'I'm just glad Mom is over it now. She told us that she had her fun, but she's happy to be back at home with us. No more running away to the circus.'

'Lucky you,' Endaria sighed. 'My mom loved the circus. She's joining it full-time, so we are **'RUNNING AWAY'** with the circus.'

'Really? That sounds awesome!'

'I'm not gonna lie, it is gonna be fun. Since your mom is quitting the trapeze, my mom wants me to learn. Mom says I have the perfect arm length for it.' Endaria held up her long Enderman arm to prove it.

'Wait,' I said after a moment. 'Does this mean that you're leaving?'

'Yeah,' Endaria sighed. 'We'll be travelling with the circus now. It was fun here while it lasted.'

'Oh,' I said slowly. I was sad Endaria was leaving. But, I realized, I wasn't devastated.

Maybe I was over my crush?

I mean, she was pretty fun to hang out with but I hadn't felt like **VOMITING** when I saw her.

OH WELL.

'I'll probably come back though,' Endaria said cheerily.

'Oh?'

'Yeah! The circus has to come back to town eventually! Although, I don't think you'll ever be invited again... Steve neither!' Endaria laughed.

I shrugged. Yeah, I think Steve and I are gonna **STEER CLEAR** of the circus for a while!

Find out what happens next in...

DIARY OF A MINECRAFT ZOMBIE

BOOK 22

ROYAL RECALL